Are You Hungry Tonight?

90 Amazing Recipes to Bring Family and Friends Together

Are You Hungry Tonight?
90 Amazing Recipes to Bring Family and Friends Together
April May Thomas © 2020

Book Production by Aloha Publishing, AlohaPublishing.com
Cover and Interior Design by Fusion Creative Works, FusionCW.com
Lead Editor: Jennifer Regner

Hardcover ISBN: 978-1-61206-227-3
Softcover ISBN: 978-1-61206-220-4

Published by

ALOHA
PUBLISHING

AlohaPublishing.com

Printed in the United States of America

To my children, Jennifer and Evan:

From my private collection of treasured recipes to warm
your heart and please the palate.
Enjoy.

A special thanks to my friend
McCarty Amy Baker:

Thank you for believing in me and encouraging me to publish.

Contents

Why I Wrote This Book

))))))))))))))))))))))

11

Measurements and Notes

✳✳✳✳✳✳✳✳✳✳✳✳✳✳✳✳✳✳

13

The Recipes

✮✮✮✮✮✮✮✮✮✮✮✮✮✮✮

About the Author

Why I Wrote This Book

My belief is we are put on this earth to enjoy lives of joy and abundance, and that is what I want for you. Cooking has always been a passion for me—it's therapy for my heart and soul. It gets me through both the tough and joyful times.

What about you? Do you love to cook? Have you cooked for years or are you just learning? I've added a "Measurements and Notes" section if you are new to cooking.

Food has always brought my children home and my friends together. *Are You Hungry Tonight?* is about bringing peace and comfort to others through making food and connecting with friends, family, and soon-to-be friends. It's about softening the stress of life and creating time for and with those you love.

Sharing recipes and watching others enjoy them is both my purpose and my passion. In our home, we value laughter and allow for tears and love, as we connect over good food made with love.

Are meals the time of day you sit around the table and reflect?

If not, will cooking and sharing what you make bring those traditions back?

Measurements and Notes

If you aren't really comfortable in the kitchen, this page is for you. Cooking isn't rocket science and what you need to know is pretty simple.

Measurements

Teaspoon

The smaller of the two measurements when using a measuring spoon (other than fractions, most commonly ¼, ½, or ¾). Some cookbooks abbreviate this as "tsp" or a lower case "t". A teaspoon can be used to measure liquid or dry ingredients.

Tablespoon

The larger of the two measurements when using a measuring spoon. One tablespoon equals three teaspoons. It's less common to see fractions of this measurement, although ½ tablespoon equals 1½ teaspoons. Some cookbooks abbreviate this as "tbsp" or a capitalized "T". A tablespoon can be used to measure liquid or dry ingredients.

Cup

Cup measures are used for both dry and liquid ingredients, although the measuring cups have different designs. For dry ingredients, measuring cups are often made of metal or plastic and should have a flat top for leveling off ingredients with a knife, if you choose to do that.

Liquid measuring cups are usually made of glass or plastic and include extra volume above the measuring lines to prevent spillage, plus a pouring lip.

One cup equals 16 tablespoons. A half cup equals 8 tablespoons.

Fluid Ounces

For measuring liquids, a fluid ounce equals 2 tablespoons. "Fluid" is used to differentiate fluid ounces from ounces by weight. A pound equals 16 ounces using a scale. Fluids are not usually weighed—they are measured by volume with measuring spoons or cups.

Ingredients by Weight

Meats, poultry, fish, cheese, butter, and produce are often measured by weight, although a volume equivalent may be included in the recipe for clarity.

Notes

Butter

Salted butter is fine to use in these recipes. For any recipe with added salt, use the amount listed as a guideline and add salt to taste as everyone has different ideas about how much is "enough."

Eggs

In most recipes, an egg means one labeled "large" in the grocery store. Use large eggs unless the recipe specifies a different-sized egg.

Flour

Use all-purpose flour when called for in these recipes.

Salt

Use whatever kind of salt you like. I often use Himalayan pink salt and sometimes use kosher salt.

The Recipes

Rosemary Walnuts

Makes 4 cups

These make wonderful "hostess gifts" and are irresistible with cocktails.

- 6 tablespoons butter
- 1 tablespoon dried rosemary, crumbled
- 3 teaspoons salt
- ½ teaspoon cayenne pepper
- 4 cups walnut halves

Melt butter in a large saucepan. Remove from heat and add seasonings. Add the walnuts and toss gently but well. Place the walnuts in a shallow roasting pan in one layer. Bake at 325°F until richly brown, about 10-15 minutes, shaking occasionally.

Very nice served warm.

Clear Japanese Soup

Serves 12

This is such a nice way to begin a dinner party.

- 3 quarts chicken broth
- ½ cup mirin (Japanese wine or dry sherry)
- 3 tablespoons soy sauce

Garnishes:

- 12-14 mushrooms, thinly sliced
- 2 lemons, thinly sliced
- 2 bunches green onions, sliced diagonally into ¼-inch thick slivers
- 1 carrot, sliced paper thin
- ½ pound tiny shrimp (optional)

Bring broth to a simmer. Stir in wine and soy sauce.
Simmer 5 minutes.

Arrange garnishes on tray. Serve broth in bowls or mugs. Have guests choose their garnishes of choice.

Curry Chicken Salad

Serves 8

The wonderful flavors in this salad need time to fully blend, so make it a day ahead.

- 2 cups mayonnaise
- 2 tablespoons lemon juice
- 1 tablespoon curry powder, rounded
- 1 tablespoon onion juice
- 1 tablespoon chutney, chopped
- 3 cups chicken or turkey, sliced
- 1½ cups celery, chopped
- 1 6-oz can sliced water chestnuts, drained
- 2 cups seedless grapes
- 1 1-pound can pineapple chunks, well drained
- ½ cup slivered almonds (toasted is okay)

Combine mayonnaise, lemon juice, soy sauce, curry powder, onion juice, and chutney. Toss mixture with remaining ingredients *except almonds*. Refrigerate overnight. Sprinkle with almonds when serving.

Serve on a bed of lettuce and artichoke hearts (optional).

This is a meal in itself.

Barbecued Teriyaki Steaks

Serves 4

Decorative and delicious, these bring a touch of refinement to barbecuing while maintaining a zesty, full-bodied flavor.

- 2 pounds flank steak
- ¾ cup olive oil
- ½ cup soy sauce
- 2 tablespoons honey
- 2 tablespoons vinegar
- 1½ teaspoons fresh ginger, finely diced
- 1 teaspoon garlic powder
- 1 scallion, finely chopped

Cut steak width-wise in ½-inch strips. Roll up each strip and secure with a toothpick.

Combine remaining ingredients with electric mixer. Marinate meat rolls in sauce for 8 hours.

With barbecue hot, grill 5 minutes each side for medium rare.

Serve with risotto (any kind). Zucchini is a nice vegetable with this and can be grilled also.

Pork Chops, Bone-In

Serves 2-4

This was my mom's recipe—and my dad's favorite.

- Olive oil
- 2-4 pork chops, center cut
- 2 onions (large), sliced thickly
- 4-6 cloves garlic, chopped and smashed
- 1 large can (1 pound and 12 oz or 28-oz can) tomato sauce
- 3 teaspoons dried oregano

Brown pork chops with a little olive oil in pan, both sides. Reduce heat to low. Place garlic on top of meat. Put extra garlic around chops in pan as this adds great flavor to sauce. Take dried oregano, crush in palms of hands, and sprinkle generously over pork chops. Top with thick slices of onion. Pour tomato sauce over chops. Cover chops completely with sauce. Place lid on pan. Cook at simmer 1½-2 hours without removing lid.

Serve with mashed potatoes, as the sauce is great on them.

These will melt in your mouth.

Cornish Game Hens

Serves 2

- 2 Cornish game hens, thawed, rinsed, and patted dry (thaw the day before)
- Butter
- Lemon, sliced
- Lime, sliced
- Fresh rosemary
- Olive oil
- Garlic salt
- Fresh pepper

Preheat oven to 350°F.

Fill cavity with slices of butter, sliced lemon, and sliced lime. Can also use fresh rosemary sprigs. Drizzle with a little olive oil inside, also all over the outside of hens. Sprinkle with garlic salt and fresh pepper.

Bake for 1 hour and 15 minutes. Can baste hens occasionally (like a turkey) by pouring juices over them while cooking.

Let stand 5 minutes before serving.

Serve with baked potato soup and sautéed asparagus in butter.

(Alternative: Can fill cavity with orange wedges instead of lemon and lime to add special flavor.)

Spaghetti and Sausage Sauce

Serves 4

- 1 1-pound roll or bulk Italian sausage, regular
- 1 1-pound roll or bulk Italian sausage, hot
- 1 large onion, diced
- 6-8 cloves garlic, smashed and diced
- 4-6 fresh Roma tomatoes, diced
- 1 package fresh basil (tube also works great)
- 1 package fresh spaghetti or linguine (find in refrigerated section)
- Fresh parmesan cheese, grated

Sauté both sausages, onion, and garlic in fry pan. Add basil and then tomatoes. Let simmer on low. I like to add tomatoes toward end, 10 minutes before serving, as I like them fresh.

Boil fresh spaghetti in salted water 1-2 minutes only. You want it al dente. Drain, place on plates, and cover with sausage sauce. Include the extra juice from cooking the sausage—it keeps the spaghetti from going dry (I love these flavors together). Sprinkle with cheese. Serve.

Chicken Baked in Roasting Bag with Vegetables

Serves 2-4

- 4-6 chicken thighs
- 3-4 chicken legs
- 1 roasting bag (Reynolds oven bags come 5 in a box and also turkey size, 2 in a box. I keep both on hand. Which one is best depends on how much you're roasting.)

Arrange roasting bag in a pan. Rub chicken pieces with olive oil. Place inside center of bag. In the corners of the bag, place any vegetable of your choice:

- Diced carrots
- Squash
- Onions
- Beets
- Brussels sprouts
- Parsnips
- Potatoes
- Mushrooms

Preheat oven to 350°F.

I like to place pats of butter on veggies to help keep them moist.

Sprinkle chicken with garlic salt. Close bag in roasting pan. Bake at 350°F for 1 hour and 10 minutes. Let stand at least 5 minutes. Serve.

(Alternative: Use pork loin instead of chicken.)

Celery with Almonds

Serves 6

If you did not like celery before, you will indeed now. This vegetable compliments seafood.

- 4 cups celery, cut in 3-inch strips
- 3 tablespoons butter
- 2 tablespoons chives, minced
- ½ cup chopped scallions with tops
- 2-3 cloves garlic, minced
- ½ cup slivered almonds

Using skillet, melt butter and add celery. Cook on low heat 3 minutes, stirring constantly. Add chives, scallions, and garlic. Sauté a bit longer, still stirring. Do not overcook. Veggies should be somewhat crisp when served. Add almonds and mix. Sprinkle top with a few almonds as a garnish.

Serve this vegetable with any fish entrée. Perfect.

Pancetta with Braised Peas

Serves 2-4

- 1 package (4-6 oz) pancetta, diced
- 1 1-pound package frozen peas
- 1 onion
- 2-4 garlic cloves
- Olive oil

Sauté in a little olive oil the pancetta, onion, and garlic. Add frozen peas last and stir to sauté. Serve immediately.

Can be served with any entrée.

Delicious flavor. Quick and easy, this is one of my favorites!

Tossed Green Salad

Serves 6-8

The secret to a great salad is crisp, cold greens. This salad is great!

- 6 tablespoons olive oil
- 2 tablespoons white wine vinegar
- ½ teaspoon salt
- 1-3 small garlic cloves
- 1 small head Boston lettuce
- 1 small head butter lettuce
- 1 small head bibb lettuce
- 3 stalks endive
- ½ bunch watercress, minus stems
- 2 tablespoons parsley, chopped
- 2 tablespoons chives, chopped
- 1 teaspoon fresh dill
- 2 teaspoons fresh thyme
- 2 teaspoons fresh tarragon
- 1 medium avocado, diced

Combine olive oil, vinegar, salt, and garlic in bottom of salad bowl. Wash lettuce leaves and tear into bite-sized pieces over dressing. Do not toss. Add watercress. Sprinkle parsley, chives, dill, thyme, and tarragon over top of lettuce. Cover with plastic wrap. Chill all day. Add avocado and then toss all salad ingredients. Serve immediately.

Fresh Berries with Belgian Chocolate Gelato

Serves 4-6

Serve in wine glasses or any elegant dish of your choice.

Slice any of:

- Strawberries
- Blueberries
- Peaches
- Pears
- Mandarin oranges

Prepared fruit can be chilled ahead of time.

- 1 container gelato (per 4 people), softened before serving

Before serving, about 30-40 minutes, remove fruit from refrigerator and scoop about one quarter of a container of gelato over each serving. Let melt at room temperature. Serve.

Very refreshing! You can use any flavor of gelato. I love Belgian chocolate flavor for this dish.

Pecan Lassies

Makes 48 tarts

This recipe was a closely guarded secret for many years. You will see why—the tarts are perfection.

Crust:

- 1 cup butter, softened
- 6 oz cream cheese, softened
- 2 cups flour

Filling:

- ½ cup butter, softened
- 1 cup sugar
- 1 egg, lightly beaten
- 1½ cups chopped pecans
- 1 cup chopped dates
- 1 tablespoon vanilla extract

Preheat oven to 350°F.

In a large bowl, add 1 cup butter, cream cheese, and flour. Mix well. Divide into 4 equal parts. Separate each part into 12 equal balls. Place balls into 4 miniature muffin tins. Using thumb, push balls into cups, working dough up sides to rim.

In another bowl, cream together filling ingredients: ½ cup butter, sugar, egg, pecans, dates, and vanilla. Divide among baking shells. Fill each shell completely.

Bake 30-40 minutes. Let cool before removing tarts. You can sprinkle tarts with powdered sugar before serving if desired.

Can be made in advance and also can be frozen. Preparation time is only 45 minutes.

Wonderful dessert for a large party.

German Pancake

Serves 2

You will need a cast-iron skillet (fry pan) to bake this in.

- 3 tablespoons butter (melt in skillet and swirl to coat)
- 3 eggs
- ½ cup flour
- ½ cup milk
- ¼ teaspoon salt
- 3 tablespoons butter (melt in microwave and set aside)

Preheat oven to 450°F.

Mix in bowl with electric mixer the eggs, flour, milk, and salt. Beat approximately 3 minutes until frothy (you need air bubbles for it to rise). Pour mixture into skillet. Pour 3 tablespoons melted butter over top of mixture and stir just slightly with a spoon. Bake at 450°F for 15 minutes.

Turn oven down to 350°F for 10 minutes (watch, as some ovens cook warmer). This will rise to a beautiful pancake. Serve with syrup.

Add on side: bacon and any fresh fruit.

Can sprinkle pancake with powdered sugar.

Just fantastic as a Sunday brunch. Pop open a bottle of prosecco!

Pistachio Cake

Serves 10-16

This is light, fluffy, and delicious. This is my children's favorite request for their birthdays.

Cake:

- 1 box yellow cake mix
- 3 eggs
- 1 cup oil
- 1 cup Seven-Up
- 1 package pistachio instant pudding (dry package)

Preheat oven to 350°F.

Mix all ingredients together with electric mixer, 3 minutes. Bake in a 9 x 13-inch glass pan or 2 round cake pans (your choice). Bake at 350°F for 30 minutes. Let cool completely.

Frosting:

- 1 package pistachio instant pudding
- 1 package Cool Whip
- ¾-1 cup milk

Combine pudding mix and Cool Whip in a bowl. Add milk slowly and beat with electric mixer to correct consistency. Spread frosting on cake. Refrigerate until ready. Serve.

I grate a Hershey's chocolate bar with a potato peeler over the top of the frosting to decorate as an extra-nice look.

Very special! Your guests will love this.

Moonlight Mellow German Chocolate Bundt Cake

Serves 16

Cake:

- 1 German chocolate cake mix
- 1-2 teaspoons cinnamon
- 1 teaspoon nutmeg
- ½ teaspoon clove (optional)
- ½ cup butter, melted
- ½ cup water
- 3 eggs
- ½ cup nuts, chopped
- 1 cup cold mashed potatoes

Glaze:

- ½ cup semisweet chocolate chips
- 1 tablespoon butter
- 2 tablespoons milk
- ½ cup powdered sugar

Preheat oven to 350°F.

Spray a Bundt pan with cooking oil. Mix all ingredients for cake with electric mixer. Stir in nuts. Bake 40-50 minutes. Cool 25 minutes.

In a saucepan, heat butter and chocolate chips, stirring, to melt. Remove. Add powdered sugar until smooth. Add a few drops of milk to smooth. Drizzle over Bundt cake.

Serves 16 people or 1 husband!

Surprise Sandwiches

Serves 6-8 for lunch

The surprise is not only how wonderful these are, but the variety of occasions they can bless. Prepare open face for lovely luncheons with champagne.

- 1 cup chicken, sliced and cooked
- ½ cup dates, finely chopped
- ¼ cup hazelnuts, chopped
- ¼ cup crisp bacon, crumbled (about 4 strips)
- ½ cup mayonnaise
- Salt (pinch)
- 12 thin slices white bread, buttered

Preheat oven to 350°F.

Dice chicken. If hazelnuts have skins, bake at 350°F for 10-15 minutes until skins split. Remove from oven, cool slightly, and rub with hands or rough towel to remove skins, then chop.

Combine all ingredients except bread. Spread on buttered bread slices, then trim crusts. Cut into desired number of triangles, either 2 (in half) for luncheon or 4 per slice of bread for tiny finger sandwiches, open face.

Absolutely superb served with any soup.

Sesame Asparagus and Shrimp

Serves 6

This is beautiful!

- 1½ pounds asparagus
- 1½ pounds medium to large raw shrimp
- ½ cup peanut oil
- 1 onion, sliced
- 4 teaspoons soy sauce
- 4 tablespoons sesame seeds
- 1 teaspoon salt
- Steamed rice for serving

Wash and trim asparagus, and cut into 2-3-inch pieces, discarding tough ends. Shell and devein shrimp.

Heat oil over medium heat in a frying pan or wok. Stir-fry asparagus, shrimp, and onion until shrimp are pink, about 3-5 minutes. Stir in soy sauce, sesame seeds, and salt. Serve over steamed rice.

Onions in Sherry

Serves 4

Just the vegetable you've been looking for to serve with grilled steaks.

- ¼ cup butter
- 5 medium onions, thinly sliced
- ½ teaspoon sugar
- 3-4 garlic cloves, smashed
- ½ teaspoon salt
- ½ teaspoon freshly ground pepper
- ½ cup dry sherry
- ¼ cup fresh parmesan cheese
- Dash of nutmeg

Sauté onions with sugar in butter on low for 30 minutes. Add smashed garlic. Sauté for an additional 5 minutes. Add dry sherry. Remove from heat and add the rest of the ingredients. Just elegant served over top of grilled steak or any meat of choice.

(Alternative: Can replace 1-2 packages sliced mushrooms, white or cremini, for the onions. Increase butter to 1-2 sticks, ½-1 cup).

Mandarin Orange Salad

Serves 6

This appealing salad can be served in a large bowl or on individual plates.

- 2 heads butter lettuce, washed and patted dry
- ½ cup celery, chopped
- ⅓ cup green onions, chopped
- ½ cup watercress
- ¼ cup parsley
- 1 11-oz can mandarin oranges, drained
- ½ cup walnuts, pecans, or pine nuts

Dressing (can be made ahead of time):

- ½ cup olive oil
- ¼ cup vinegar
- 2 tablespoons sugar
- ½ teaspoon Worcestershire sauce
- 1 teaspoon salt
- Pepper
- Dash of Tabasco sauce

Mix well or shake in bottle. Chill. Dress salad when serving.

Delicious substitutions for the mandarin oranges are grapefruit or avocado slices.

Spinach Salad

Serves 4-6

- 1 bunch spinach
- 6 slices bacon
- 3 tablespoons bacon drippings
- 2 tablespoons orange juice
- 2 tablespoons cider vinegar
- 2 tablespoons currant jelly
- ½ cup sliced almonds or pine nuts

Rinse and dry spinach. Tear into bite-sized pieces in salad bowl. Fry bacon until crisp. Drain on paper towel and slice thin when cool. Reserve 3 tablespoons bacon drippings in skillet. Add orange juice, vinegar, and jelly to skillet. Bring to a boil before serving and pour over spinach. Toss with bacon and almonds.

Light-as-a-Feather Corn Bread

Serves 6

The rye flour gives this a marvelously nutty flavor quality. It's great for barbecues, with heavy stew, or at breakfast with sausage or bacon.

- ¾ cup white flour, unsifted
- ¾ cup rye flour, unsifted
- ½ cup corn meal
- 3 teaspoons baking powder
- Pinch of salt
- 2 eggs
- ½ cup sugar
- ½ cup melted butter
- 1 cup milk

Heat oven to 425°F.

Prepare 9-inch baking dish by greasing it or spraying it with Pam. Combine dry ingredients except sugar in a bowl. Set aside.

In large bowl, beat eggs and sugar. Add melted butter. With wooden spoon, mix in dry ingredients, alternating with milk. Pour into baking dish. Bake 20 minutes.

Hootsla

Serves 4

An irresistible Pennsylvanian Dutch version of French toast that somehow made it (thankfully) to the West Coast. Warm applesauce and sausage are a must with this.

- ½ loaf of day-old sourdough or French bread
- ½ cup butter
- 3 eggs
- ½ cup milk
- Salt and pepper

Cut bread, crust and all, into cubes. Melt butter in large skillet. Add bread cubes and brown, stirring.

Beat eggs until light colored then combine with milk and salt and pepper. Remove bread from heat. Pour egg/milk mixture over bread. Return to heat and stir constantly until egg is entirely cooked.

Serve immediately with maple syrup.

Lemon Dainty Dessert

Serves 6

This was found neatly penned on a tattered page of an old family recipe book that belonged to my grandmother. The date was 1931. The description: " . . . a delicate crust will form on top of pudding . . . supplies its own sauce. Very fine." It is a very fine pudding cake. Pretty, simple, and refreshing.

- 1 cup sugar
- ¼ cup flour
- ⅛ teaspoon salt
- 2 tablespoons melted butter
- 5-6 tablespoons lemon juice
- Grated rind of 2 small lemons
- 3 egg yolks
- 1½ cups milk
- 3 egg whites

Heat oven to 350°F.

Combine dry ingredients in large bowl. Add melted butter, lemon juice, and rind. Blend. Add yolks and milk and beat together well. Beat egg whites until stiff but not dry. Fold into lemon mixture. Pour into quart dish. Set dish inside roasting pan and fill with 1 inch of hot water. Bake 1 hour.

Can be served hot or cold in shallow bowls.

This is lovely with fresh berries.

Pumpkin Bars

Serves 12

These are great during any time of the year. They can be dessert or appetizer. Great at potlucks or get-togethers.

- 4 eggs
- 1⅔ cups sugar
- 1 16-oz can pumpkin
- 2 cups flour
- 2 teaspoons baking powder
- 2 teaspoons cinnamon
- 1 teaspoon salt
- 1 teaspoon baking soda

Preheat oven to 350°F.

Mix all ingredients in large bowl. Spread mixture onto cookie sheet with short sides around edges, not a flat sheet. Bake for 25 minutes. Let cool.

Icing:

- 3 oz cream cheese
- ½ cup butter
- 1 teaspoon vanilla
- 2 cups powdered sugar

Mix all ingredients until smooth. Can be chilled until pumpkin bars are ready to slice into squares and serve, or kept at room temperature.

Your guests will love these. I make these during the holidays a lot.

These will disappear!

Favorite Milkshake

Serves 1-2

This is very refreshing at home, for enjoying from your deck on a fabulously sunny day.

- 2 cups vanilla ice cream
- ½ oz crème de cacao
- ½ oz brandy
- ½ oz Kahlua

Put ice cream in blender. Pour in liqueurs. Blend until the consistency is like a milkshake. Serve in chilled glasses from freezer.

Irish Coffee

Serves 2-3

- Hot brewed coffee
- 1 jigger (1oz) Kahlua
- 1 jigger (1oz) Amaretto
- 1 jigger (1oz) vodka
- Whipping cream

Fill mugs half full with coffee. Blend liqueurs and vodka together and divide between mugs. Top with whipped cream.

Very good.

Soups Are Great with Any Meal

Serves 2

So here is my secret: I used to spend hours preparing homemade soups from scratch. Not only is it costly, but you can now buy them from Safeway Signature Soups. One large container feeds two people. They are made fresh daily.

My favorite flavors:

- Butternut Squash
- Baked Potato Soup
- Tomato Basil Tuscan Style
- White Bean and Kale
- Clam Chowder
- Broccoli Cheesy Cheddar
- Stompin' Beef Chili

The good news: I hope Tom knows he can now have soup anytime. Oh-la-la!

Southern Boneless Baked Chicken Breasts

Serves 8

This recipe is from Ozark, Alabama. It has a most elegant and fantastic flavor. It's a very special dinner. You can prepare it ahead and put it in the oven before your guests arrive. Your house will smell liked you cooked for hours.

- 8 boneless, skinless chicken breasts
- 1 jar Armour dried beef (can be found by Spam in stores)
- 2 cans cream of mushroom soup
- 8 oz sour cream
- 8 slices of bacon, uncooked

Preheat oven to 275°F. Prepare baking dish by spraying with Pam or olive oil.

Roll chicken breasts and wrap bacon around middle. Secure with a toothpick. Take dried beef and chop and dice into small bite-sized pieces. Sprinkle over bottom of prepared pan. Place each rolled chicken on top. Combine soup and sour cream and pour over chicken.

Bake for 3 hours, uncovered.

Can be served with rice. Sauce is great over rice and chicken. This dish is great with asparagus or a fresh light salad.

Melts in your mouth!

Au Gratin Potatoes

Serves 6

"This is so elegant."

"Tastes like decadence."

We made this a family tradition for Christmas Day. It can be served with any meal. I have seen guests be speechless after tasting this dish.

- 6-8 Yukon Gold or russet potatoes
- 1 stick butter, cold
- ½ carton whipping cream (not half-and-half)
- 2-3 leeks, chopped and washed well—dirt hides between leaves
- 1 Gruyère cheese block, grated and ready to sprinkle (3-5 oz, can be found at Trader Joe's)

Preheat oven to 350°F.

Choose your baking dish size according to number of guests. Grease the bottom of dish well with cold butter. Peel potatoes as you go (2-3 at a time). Slice on large grater lengthwise so rounds are paper thin. Layer on bottom. Pour ⅓ of the whipping cream over potatoes. Sprinkle ⅓ of leeks over whipping cream. Add salt and pepper. Sprinkle ⅓ of the cheese over leeks. Repeat 2-3 times. Bake for 2 hours, covered with foil. Uncover for the last 15 minutes to brown. Let stand 5 minutes. Cut into squares and serve with entrée.

Fantastic the next day as leftovers!

Baked Prime Rib Roast

Serves 4-6

- Beef prime rib roast, bone-in
- 8-10 cloves garlic
- ½ cup balsamic vinegar
- ¼-½ cup olive oil
- 4 tablespoons cracked fresh pepper
- 1½ teaspoons salt
- ½ cup Dijon mustard, whole grain

Preheat oven to 450°F.

Blend all ingredients except roast. Put roast and mixture in large roasting bag. Close bag. Work mixture into roast. Let stand 2-8 hours in refrigerator.

Bake in large, deep roasting pan at 450°F for 30 minutes exactly.

Reduce heat to 300°F and cook 15 minutes per pound more.

Meat thermometer: 125-135°F = rare

135-140°F = medium rare

140-150°F = medium-medium well

Let stand 10-15 minutes before carving.

Your butcher can section and trim ribs and tie together with string to bake.

Just an excellent choice. Great for holidays and special occasions!

Rack of Lamb with Mustard, Lemon, and Herbs

Serves 4

- 2 racks of lamb
- 2 teaspoons butter, melted
- 4 tablespoons breadcrumbs
- 2 tablespoons Dijon mustard
- 2 tablespoons fresh marjoram, basil, mint, or parsley, chopped
- Grated rind of 2 small lemons

Toss melted butter with breadcrumbs. Add fresh herbs and lemon rind.

Coat back of lamb with mustard. Firmly press on herbed breadcrumbs.

Ways to cook:

Oven: Bake at 400°F for 20 minutes for rare, 25 minutes for medium. Remove and let stand 5 minutes before serving.

Grill: Cook on grill 10 minutes each side. Cook herbed side last. Let sit 5 minutes on platter before serving.

Serve with tiny potatoes or mashed potatoes.

Parmesan Crusted Chicken

Serves 4

- 4 boneless chicken breasts
- ½ cup mayonnaise
- ¼ cup fresh parmesan cheese, grated
- 4 teaspoons Italian seasoned breadcrumbs

Preheat oven to 425°F.

Combine mayonnaise with cheese. Arrange chicken on baking sheet. Top with mayonnaise mixture and breadcrumbs. Bake 20 minutes.

This chicken will be juicy and delicious.

Moist and Crispy Onion Chicken

Serves 3-4

- 1 envelope Lipton Onion Soup and Dip Mix
- ¾ cup Italian seasoned breadcrumbs
- 2½-3½ pounds of chicken (a mix of legs, thighs, breasts on bone)
- ½ cup mayonnaise

Preheat oven to 400°F.

Place onion soup mix and breadcrumbs in large plastic food bag and shake to blend.

Brush chicken on all sides with mayonnaise. Place one piece of chicken in bag at a time, close, and shake to coat. Place chicken in baking pan.

Bake for 40-45 minutes or until golden brown.

For extra oniony chicken, use 2 envelopes of Lipton Onion Soup Mix and reduce breadcrumbs to ⅓ cup.

Sometimes I use panko instead of breadcrumbs. Either works fine.

Avocado and Mushroom Piquant

Serves 8

This has a lovely charm. A tasty first course.

- 2 avocados
- ½ pound small mushrooms
- ½ cup oil
- 3 tablespoons tarragon vinegar
- 2 tablespoons lemon juice
- 2 tablespoons water
- 1 tablespoon parsley, chopped
- 2 cloves garlic, finely minced
- ¾ teaspoon salt
- Freshly ground pepper

Peel and slice avocados. Remove stems from mushrooms. Place in bowl to chill and refrigerate 3 hours.

Blend remaining ingredients and pour over avocados and mushrooms. Chill several hours (at least 3), spooning the dressing over vegetables several times.

Serve over attractive lettuce leaves on small plates. Excellent served with steak or salmon.

Gazpacho

Serves 6

- 1 large tomato, peeled
- ½ small onion
- ½ cucumber
- ½ green pepper
- 1 large stalk celery
- 2 teaspoons parsley, chopped
- 1 teaspoon chives, chopped
- 2 cloves garlic, minced fine
- 2 cups tomato vegetable juice (V8 is great)
- 2-3 tablespoons red wine vinegar
- 2 tablespoons olive oil
- 1 tablespoon lemon juice
- 1 teaspoon sugar
- 1 teaspoon salt
- ¼ teaspoon white pepper
- ½ teaspoon Worcestershire sauce
- ⅛ teaspoon Tabasco sauce

Finely chop all vegetables (a food processor is ideal for this). Combine and refrigerate at least 2 hours. Serve in chilled bowls and pass an assortment of garnishes: chopped hard boiled eggs, chopped green onions, bacon bits, croutons, chopped avocados, and more.

This is the best you have ever had!

Fettuccini Ferrari

Serves 4-6

Nice! You may treat this as a first course or an entrée. Serve with salad and French bread. The cherry tomatoes give it extra appeal for a summer supper.

- 1 pound fresh fettuccini
- ½ cup butter
- 1 bunch green onions, chopped
- 2 cloves garlic, minced (more if desired)
- 1 cup cherry tomatoes, quartered
- 4 oz ham or porchetta or pancetta, diced
- 1 egg yolk
- ¼ cup heavy cream
- ½ cup freshly grated parmesan cheese
- Salt
- Freshly ground pepper

Melt butter in skillet. Add onion and garlic and cook until tender. Add tomatoes and cook 1-2 minutes. Add ham and cook until heated through. Beat egg yolk and then beat heavy cream into the egg until well mixed. Add remaining ingredients (egg and cream, cheese, salt, and pepper). Cook gently until heated through.

In large kettle, boil fettuccini for 2 minutes. Drain. Add hot sauce to fettuccini and serve immediately.

Spaghetti Carbonara

Serves 6-8

Great for dinner in ski country or on a cold rainy night.

- 8 slices of thick-sliced bacon, cut into tiny pieces
- 1 large onion, thinly sliced
- ¼ cup dry white wine
- 3 eggs, lightly beaten
- ¾ cup fresh grated parmesan cheese
- 2 tablespoons parsley, chopped
- ½ teaspoon salt
- Freshly cracked pepper
- 1 pound fresh spaghetti or linguine
- Freshly grated parmesan cheese (for topping)

In skillet, lightly brown bacon pieces and onion. Pour off all but ½ cup bacon drippings. Add white wine. Simmer 10-15 minutes. Then in a bowl, combine eggs, parmesan cheese, parsley, salt, and pepper. Next, cook spaghetti in boiling water 2 minutes, until just "al dente." Drain.

Toss hot spaghetti with egg mixture. Add bacon mixture. Serve pasta immediately on plates or in big pasta bowl. Have extra grated cheese on hand. Serve warm!

Delicious.

Sole Inge-Lise

Serves 8

A beautiful, simple, and delicious fish course.

- 3 pounds small fillets of sole
- Salt and white pepper
- ½ pound tiny shrimp
- 1 cup chopped leeks
- 1 tablespoon butter
- 1 cup heavy whipping cream (liquid from carton)
- 4-5 tablespoons tomato paste
- 2½ tablespoons Dijon wine mustard
- 1½ teaspoons cornstarch

Preheat oven to 350°F.

Season fillets with salt and white pepper. Spoon shrimp onto the fillets and roll up. Place them together in buttered casserole dish.

Sauté leeks in butter until limp and spoon over fillets. Next, combine tomato paste, cream, mustard, and cornstarch until well blended. Pour over leeks and fish. Can be refrigerated until ready to bake. Let reach room temperature before baking. Bake uncovered at 350°F for 30 minutes. Serve as entree with fresh bread or fluffy white rice. Add a vegetable on the side (like celery with almonds).

Fillet of Sole West Indies

Serves 4

A quite different and nicely exotic sole. Very elegant!

- 4 medium fillets of sole (about 1½ pounds)
- ¼ cup flour
- 1 teaspoon salt
- ¼ teaspoon white pepper
- 1 teaspoon paprika
- ⅓ cup butter
- ½ cup dry white wine
- ½ teaspoon ginger
- 2 tablespoons lemon juice
- 2 tablespoons brown sugar
- 2 bananas, cut in quarters lengthwise
- 2-3 oz slivered almonds (optional)

Dip fillets in mixture of flour, paprika, salt, and pepper. In skillet, melt butter and brown fillets for 2-3 minutes on each side. Remove to platter. Then, combine wine, ginger, lemon juice, and brown sugar in skillet. Add bananas and heat on medium. Cook 2 minutes, spooning sauce over bananas.

Pour sauce with bananas over fillets. Sprinkle with almonds.

Keep the rest of your menu simple: fluffy white rice and a fresh green vegetable or crisp cold salad.

Rosemary Leg of Lamb

Serves 6

This tastes as superb as its aroma smells.

- 1 leg of lamb, well trimmed of fat
- Salt
- ¼ cup parsley, finely chopped
- 3 tablespoons fresh rosemary, diced
- 1 tablespoon olive oil
- 2 cloves garlic, smashed and crushed (I always double my garlic and love it!)
- ¼ teaspoon salt
- 1¼ cups chicken broth
- Potatoes for roasting alongside the lamb, if desired

Preheat oven to 325°F.

Rub entire leg with salt. With small knife, make 6-7 deep incisions into the thickest part of the meat.

Combine the rest of remaining ingredients except broth. Gently push mixture into incisions with fingers and handle of a teaspoon. Spread any leftover mixture over surface of meat.

Roast 2½ hours, basting frequently with chicken broth.

Place peeled and diced potatoes around leg of lamb in pan 1 hour before it's done. Turn potatoes once during their roasting time.

Mushrooms au Gratin

Serves 8

This dish is wonderfully delicious but very rich, so be cautious in your menu planning. I suggest grilled meats or simple chicken entrées and a green vegetable such as shredded zucchini.

- 2 pounds mushrooms, sliced
- 1 tablespoon butter
- ⅔ cup sour cream
- 2 tablespoons flour
- ½ teaspoon salt
- ⅛ teaspoon freshly ground pepper
- 1 cup chopped parsley
- 1 cup shredded Gruyère or Swiss cheese

Preheat oven to 425°F.

Sauté mushrooms in butter for 1 minute, stirring. Cover and cook gently until juicy, 3 to 5 minutes. In bowl, blend sour cream, flour, salt, and pepper. Stir gently into mushrooms and boil. Remove from heat and immediately pour into baking dish. Combine parsley and cheese. Sprinkle on top of the dish. Bake uncovered for 10 minutes.

Except for the baking step, this can be prepared ahead of time.

Shredded Zucchini

Serves 6

Zucchini becomes elegant!

- 6 small zucchini
- 2 tablespoons butter
- 6 green onions, chopped
- Salt and pepper
- Freshly ground nutmeg
- Parmesan cheese (optional)

Shred zucchini. Use the food processor with a coarse shredding disk, or by hand with a grater on the larger holes. Drain on paper towels. Place zucchini in skillet with butter and green onions. Toss mixture until just heated through. Remove from heat and season with salt, pepper, and nutmeg.

Serve immediately. Sprinkle with Parmesan cheese if you wish.

Tomatoes Filled with Green Pasta

Serves 8

The beautiful colors make this a striking vegetable dish. It is good for a buffet. It is also nice as a pasta dish or served with steak.

- ¼ pound spinach egg noodles
- 8 medium-sized tomatoes
- Salt and pepper
- 1 cup heavy cream
- 1 cup light cream
- ½ teaspoon ground thyme
- ½ teaspoon salt
- ⅛ teaspoon white pepper
- Freshly grated Parmesan cheese

Preheat oven to 350°F.

Cook noodles in water according to package directions until firm and "al dente." Cut tops off the tomatoes and scoop out the insides (reserve fresh for sauce or add to soups or omelets.) Season inside of tomatoes with salt and pepper. Set aside. Heat both creams in saucepan and season with thyme, salt, and pepper. Add drained noodles and simmer gently until liquid is absorbed, about 15 minutes, stirring occasionally. Add salt if needed. Place tomatoes on baking sheet. Bake five minutes. Fill tomato shells with noodles and bake 3 to 4 minutes more. Sprinkle with cheese and serve.

Carrots in Mint Sauce

Serves 4

This is lovely with veal, lamb, or chicken. Carrots lend that perfect touch of color. The lemon is the secret touch! If you wish, prepare carrots and sauce well ahead of time, but do not combine until ready to serve.

- Six carrots, diced, sliced, or slivered
- ⅓ cup reserved liquid (from carrots)
- 2 tablespoons butter
- 1 tablespoon sugar
- 1 teaspoon cornstarch
- ⅛ teaspoon salt
- Juice and grated rind from ½ lemon
- 1 teaspoon finely chopped mint leaves

Parboil carrots in covered saucepan in a small amount of salted water for 4 to 8 minutes. Cook until barely tender. Remove carrots and reserve ⅓ cup of cooking liquid. To make the sauce, melt butter in saucepan. Combine sugar, cornstarch, and salt. Stir into butter. Add remaining ingredients and reserved liquid. Stir until thickened. When ready to serve, add carrots to heated sauce and toss to glaze. Serve warm.

Wild Rice Salad

Serves 6-8

Serve at picnics or parties with an abundance of butter lettuce leaves heaped in a napkin-lined basket. Instruct your guest to place a spoonful of the salad on a lettuce leaf, then roll up to eat as a sandwich.

- 1 cup wild rice
- 1¼ cups chicken broth
- 1 clove garlic
- 1 bunch of scallions, chopped
- 3 tablespoons butter
- 1 cup chopped mushrooms (½ pound)
- 3 strips bacon, diced and fried crispy
- ½ cup Greek olives with pimento
- ⅓ cup olive oil
- 3 tablespoons white wine vinegar with tarragon
- ½ teaspoon dried marjoram
- Salt and pepper to taste
- Butter lettuce leaves for serving

Soak rice in water overnight. Rinse then simmer, covered, in chicken broth with whole garlic clove until liquid is absorbed, 20 to 25 minutes. Rice will be dry but fluffy. Discard garlic.

In sauté pan, sauté scallions and then add mushrooms. Add to rice along with all remaining ingredients. Toss. Season with salt and pepper and chill for 24 hours.

Serve cold, tossing once more. Note: rice can also be served in tomato shells—refer to recipe with green pasta.

Unique and delicious!

Forest Berries with Orange Cream

Serves 4

A simple but most pleasing summer treat. Do notice the nice variations.

- 1 pint strawberries
- 1 tablespoon sugar
- ½ cup sugar
- 2 teaspoons grated orange rind
- ½ cup orange juice
- 1 cup heavy cream

Wash and hull berries. Cut in half. Combine with 1 tablespoon sugar and set aside. Next, combine ½ cup sugar, orange rind, and orange juice in a small saucepan. Bring to a boil, stirring only until sugar dissolves. Simmer 10 minutes without stirring. Cool completely. Whip cream until soft peaks form, using electric mixer. Gently fold in orange syrup. Serve over berries.

Variations: substitute fresh blueberries or raspberries and instead of orange, use lemon juice and rind in the same quantities.

Top Ramen Coleslaw

Serves 6-8

From my St. Lewis, Washington, army wives' cookbook. Great for barbecues. One of my favorite salads.

Dressing:

- 1 tablespoon sugar
- ½ teaspoon salt
- ½ cup olive oil
- 3 tablespoons rice vinegar
- ½ teaspoon white pepper
- Seasoning from Top Ramen package

Mix all together and chill.

Salad mixings:

- ½ cabbage, shredded (I like to use ¼ green and ¼ purple)
- 2 tablespoons sesame seeds, can be toasted
- ¼ cup slivered almonds, can be toasted
- 4 green onions, chopped
- One package Top Ramen, chicken flavored—dry noodles, crumbled

Pour dressing all together over salad. Let stand for one hour. Chill until served.

Frozen Fruit Salad

Serves 4-6

- 1 can cherry pie filling
- 1 small can crushed pineapple, drained
- 1 banana, mashed or cubed
- 1 teaspoon lemon juice
- 1 can sweetened condensed milk
- 1 large container (16 oz) Cool Whip

Mix fruits with lemon juice. Add condensed milk. Stir in Cool Whip and mix well.

Freeze in a covered container for one hour.

Stuffed Cherry Tomatoes

How lucky you are! Both of these are so good there is no way to choose, so here are both versions.

Hollow out 36 cherry tomatoes and turn upside down to drain on paper towels.

Bacon Filling:

- ½ pound bacon, chopped
- 8 green onions, chopped fine
- ½ cup mayonnaise

Fry bacon until crisp and drain well. Mix in green onions and mayonnaise. Stuff tomatoes and chill.

Or

Crab filling:

- 1 cup shredded cooked crab
- ¼ cup fresh lime juice
- 3 oz cream cheese, softened
- ¼ cup cream
- 2 tablespoons mayonnaise
- 1 tablespoon minced onions
- ½ teaspoon minced garlic
- 1 teaspoon dill weed, chopped or dried
- 1 teaspoon Worcestershire sauce
- 2 drops Tabasco sauce
- Salt to taste

Marinate crab in lime juice for one hour. Drain well. Combine all other ingredients and then add crab last. Fill tomatoes and chill.

Gullixson Crab

Serves 8-10

This is a smashing hors d'oeuvre for those of us who never seem to have enough time in the day to prepare such good things!

- 1 small onion or one bunch green onions
- 12 oz cream cheese, softened
- 1 tablespoon butter, softened
- 1 tablespoon Worcestershire sauce
- 1 tablespoon lemon juice
- 6 oz bottled seafood sauce
- 1½ tablespoons prepared horseradish
- ½ pound seafood (crabmeat or coarsely chopped shrimp)
- Watercress or parsley
- Crackers or Melba toast for serving

Combine onion, cream cheese, butter, Worcestershire sauce, and lemon juice (a food processor does this beautifully). Spread into a 1-inch thick circle or square on an attractive platter. Combine seafood sauce and horseradish and pour over cheese mixture. Top with seafood and garnish (I use parsley). Chill until ready to serve. Serve with thin crackers or Melbas.

Halibut with Rosemary

Serves 4

Understatement is what makes this so special.

- 1½ pounds halibut steaks
- Juice of 2-3 limes
- Salt and pepper
- 2 tablespoons olive oil
- ¼ cup white wine vinegar
- 2 tablespoons water
- 3 cloves garlic, lightly pounded
- ½ teaspoon rosemary, crushed

In glass dish, marinate halibut in lime juice for 1 to 2 hours. Wipe with paper towels. Sprinkle with salt and pepper and dredge with flour, shaking off excess. Heat oil in skillet until it ripples. Add fish and brown on both sides, about five minutes per side. Transfer to platter and cover with foil.

Add vinegar and water to pan drippings. When sizzling stops, add garlic and rosemary. Simmer until reduced to half, stirring and scraping to blend. Discard garlic cloves. Spoon mixture over fish.

Garlic Chicken

Serves 4

Think of this for an intimate supper for four. Serve with a wonderful jug of wine.

- 1 chicken, quartered
- 3 tablespoons oil
- ½ teaspoon thyme
- ½ teaspoon oregano
- ½ teaspoon savory
- 1 bouquet garnish of parsley, celery, bay leaf, and leek
- 4 heads garlic, unpeeled

Preheat oven to 350°F.

Wash and thoroughly dry chicken. Place in an earthenware casserole that has a lid. Add oil, thyme, oregano, and savory, then turn chicken pieces to coat well. Tie together in large bouquet parsley sprigs, a small celery stalk or two, a bay leaf, and a small leek, root and all. Place in center of casserole dish and surround with chicken. Break apart garlic heads and place unpeeled cloves all around. Make a paste with ⅓ cup flour, 2-3 tablespoons water, and teaspoon or so of oil. Place lid on casserole and seal with the paste. Bake for 1½ hours.

The fun is in not breaking the seal. Delight your guests with delicious smells. Just push garlic aside when serving.

Serve with potatoes.

Veal Picante

Serves 6-8

This menu is a harried hostess's dream. It may be prepared many hours ahead to create an exquisite dinner.

- 2 pounds veal scallops (small cutlets)
- Flour
- ½ cup butter
- ½ cup dry white wine
- ¼ cup lemon juice
- 1 clove garlic, minced
- Salt and pepper to taste
- ½ pound mushrooms, sliced
- 1 bunch green onions, finely sliced
- Parsley, chopped

Preheat oven to 350°F.

Dredge veal scallops in flour, shaking off excess. In skillet, melt butter over medium heat. Brown veal in batches, sautéing one minute per side.

Returning all meat to pan, add wine, lemon juice, garlic, salt, and pepper. Reduce heat to medium and cook 1 minute. At this point everything may be transferred to a casserole dish and refrigerated. Let veal return to room temperature before baking. Top with sliced mushrooms and green onions.

Bake at 350°F for 30 minutes. Sprinkle with parsley before serving.

Grits Soufflé

Serves 8

This soufflé is just different enough to make it tops! Excellent substitute for potatoes or rice and holds very well.

- 1 quart milk
- 1 cup quick-cooking grits
- ½ cup butter
- 1½ teaspoons salt
- ⅛ teaspoon cayenne pepper
- 3 (generous) cups shredded Jarlsberg cheese
- 6 eggs, well beaten

Preheat oven to 350°F.

In skillet, bring milk to boil and stir in grits with a whisk. Reduce heat and continue stirring until it becomes a thick mush, approximately 3 to 4 minutes. Remove from heat. Add butter in pieces, salt, cayenne pepper, and cheese, beating well with wooden spoon. Beat in eggs. Pour into casserole dish and bake uncovered for 1 hour and 10 minutes or until well puffed and golden brown.

This recipe can be cut in half. Bake 45 to 50 minutes. If you wish to make this ahead, you may prepare everything except the eggs, refrigerate overnight, and add the eggs in the morning.

Apricot and Pine Nut Pilaf

Serves 4-6

The perfect companion to lamb and pork.

- ¼ cup pine nuts
- ¼ cup butter
- 1 onion, chopped
- 1 cup white rice
- 1¾ cups chicken broth
- ½ cup chopped dried apricots
- 2 tablespoons butter (optional)

In saucepan, brown pine nuts with butter over medium heat. With slotted spoon, remove nuts and reserve.

Sauté onion and brown butter until soft and then add rice. Sauté for 1-2 minutes before adding chicken broth. Bring to a boil. Reduce heat and simmer, covered, for 20 minutes or until most of chicken stock is absorbed. Add apricots and reserved pine nuts. Cook an additional 10 minutes. Toss with butter just before serving.

Italian Potatoes

Serves 6

There is no question this is a man's favorite recipe both in origin and appeal. Just right for barbecues or with hearty meats. It may be prepared ahead except for the addition of oil.

- 4 large russet potatoes
- ½ cup fine breadcrumbs
- ½ cup fresh grated Parmesan cheese
- 2-3 large tomatoes, finely sliced
- 2 large red onions, thinly sliced
- ½ teaspoon oregano
- 1½ teaspoons salt
- Freshly ground pepper
- ½-¾ cup olive oil

Preheat oven to 350°F.

Peel and cut potatoes lengthwise into wedges, about 6 to 8 per potato. Drop into bowl of cold water. Next, combine breadcrumbs and cheese. Do not dry wedges before coating them well with the crumb mixture. Place in baking dish and sprinkle any remaining crumbs on top.

Top potatoes with sliced tomatoes and onion rings. Sprinkle with oregano, salt, and pepper. Drizzle with oil just before baking. Bake uncovered for 1 hour and 10 minutes, until potatoes are browned but maintain their crunchiness.

Sicilian Broccoli

Serves 4-6

- 1½ pounds broccoli
- ¼ pound butter
- 1 clove garlic, minced
- ½ teaspoon anchovy paste
- Juice of 1 lemon
- Salt and pepper to taste

Steam the broccoli until crisp tender. In saucepan, melt butter over medium heat and add garlic and anchovy paste. Blend with a whisk and let gently simmer for a minute or two. Add lemon juice, salt, and pepper. Pour over cooked broccoli.

This simple dish is so good.

Sour Cream Coffee Cake

Serves 12

The lightest and loveliest of all the coffee cakes we have ever tasted. The secret is in the proportions of the ingredients, and "cake flour" is a must.

- ½ pound butter, softened
- 2 cups sugar
- 2 eggs
- ½ teaspoon vanilla
- 1 cup sour cream
- 1¾ cups of flour, "cake flour" only
- 1 teaspoon baking powder
- ¼ teaspoon salt
- ½ cup chopped pecans or walnuts
- 2 tablespoons dark brown sugar
- 1½ teaspoons cinnamon

Preheat oven to 350°F.

Butter a Bundt pan or tube pan. In a large bowl, cream together butter and sugar. Add eggs, one at a time, beating well after each addition. Add vanilla and sour cream and blend. Sift together cake flour, baking powder, and salt in a separate bowl. Stir into sour cream mixture. Combine nuts, brown sugar, and cinnamon. Spoon half of batter into pan. Sprinkle with half of nut mixture. Cover with rest of batter and then with the remaining nut mixture. Bake 1 hour. Cool. Carefully remove from pan, placing cake upright so topping is still on top (do not flip upside down).

Papa's Favorite Torte

Serves 12

It became increasingly difficult to find an appropriate gift for Papa, so one holiday I treated him to this wonderful almond torte. It's been his special Christmas present ever since.

Crust:

- ½ cup flour
- 5 tablespoons sugar
- ½ cup butter, softened
- 1 egg yolk, lightly beaten (save the white for filling, below)

Preheat oven to 325°F.

In bowl, combine flour and sugar. Using a pastry blender or two table knives, cut in butter until evenly mixed. Stir in egg yolk. Appearance will be crumbly. Using your fingers, press pastry mixture into a tart pan with a removable bottom, working it evenly over bottom and up sides.

Filling:

- 8 oz almond paste, crumbled
- 2 tablespoons sugar
- 2 tablespoons flour
- 2 eggs
- 1 egg white
- ½ teaspoon almond extract

Place almond paste, sugar, flour, and two eggs in an electric blender or food processor. Blend until smooth. Add egg white and almond extract. Blend again, and then pour into pastry shell. Bake 1 hour at 325°F until top is golden brown. Cool 10 minutes before glazing.

Glaze:

- ½ cup sliced almonds
- 1 cup powdered sugar
- 2 tablespoons milk

While torte is cooling, spread almonds on a greased cookie sheet and toast in oven at 325°F for 10 minutes, or until lightly browned. Combine powdered sugar and milk and spread over torte. Sprinkle with almonds. When cool, remove from pan and serve in small slices.

This keeps beautifully!

Bread Pudding with Apples

Serves 8

If there are those who do not care for bread pudding, this may change their mind. The apples lend special flavor and texture, making this an ideal fall dessert.

- 1½ pounds baking apples, green
- ½ cup butter, divided in half
- 2 tablespoons sugar
- ¼ teaspoon cinnamon
- 1 1-pound loaf of French bread
- ¼ cup seedless raisins
- 4 eggs
- 1 quart milk
- ⅔ cup sugar
- 2 teaspoons vanilla
- Grating of nutmeg
- Lightly whipped cream (optional)

Preheat oven to 325°F.

Peel, core, and cut apples into large dice. Melt ¼ cup butter in a large skillet. Add apples, sprinkling with 2 tablespoons sugar and the cinnamon. Sauté over medium heat for 10 minutes, stirring frequently. Remove crusts from bread and cut into ½ inch cubes. Soften the remaining ¼ cup butter and liberally grease baking dish and add leftover butter to the bread cubes, cutting into bits.

Combine bread, raisins, apples, and the pan juices in the baking dish.

Combine eggs, milk, sugar, vanilla, and nutmeg, beating lightly with a whisk. Pour over bread and apples.

Set dish in a shallow pan filled with 1 inch of warm water. Bake for 1½ hours or until set. This may take up to 2 hours, depending on the type of casserole.

Serve hot with lightly whipped cream.

Cream Cheese Nut Cookies

Makes 3 dozen

A special cookie for special occasions.

- 1 cup sifted flour
- ½ cup butter, softened
- 3 oz cream cheese, softened
- ⅓ cup chopped nuts
- 2 tablespoons sugar
- ¼ teaspoon vanilla
- Powdered sugar

Preheat oven to 400°F.

Combine flour, butter, and cream cheese. Chill. Roll out to ⅛-inch thickness. Cut into circles (about 2½ inches).

Combine remaining ingredients except powdered sugar. Place a teaspoon or so of nut mixture in each circle of dough. Fold over, pressing edges with a fork to seal. Bake 10 minutes on ungreased cookie sheets. While hot, roll in powdered sugar.

Chocolate Snowballs

Makes 4 dozen

Dainty cookies to grace a tea luncheon or holiday tray.

- 1 cup butter, softened
- ⅔ cup powdered sugar
- 2 tablespoons cocoa
- 1½ cups sifted flour
- 1 teaspoon vanilla
- ½ cup chopped nuts (optional)
- Powdered sugar

Preheat oven to 350°F.

With an electric beater, cream together butter, sugar, and cocoa. Beat in flour, then vanilla and nuts. Form into 1-inch balls (the dough will be rather soft) and bake on ungreased cookie sheet for 15 minutes. Sift powdered sugar over cookies when cool.

Pork Tenderloin with Pumpkin Seed Pesto

Serves 4

- 2 pounds pork tenderloin
- ¾ teaspoon salt
- ¼ teaspoon ground pepper
- 1½ teaspoons olive oil
- 2 garlic cloves
- ¼ small onion, coarsely chopped
- ½ cup chicken broth
- ¼ cup roasted, salted, and shelled pumpkin seeds
- 3 tablespoons fresh cilantro leaves
- ½ teaspoon ground cumin

Preheat oven to 400°F.

Sprinkle both sides of pork with salt and pepper. In a skillet, add 1 teaspoon oil. Brown pork 4-6 minutes, turning once. Place in a roasting pan and roast for 20 to 25 minutes. Place pork on cutting board and loosely cover with foil. Let stand 15 minutes before slicing. Meanwhile, in food processor with knife blade, purée garlic, onion, broth, pumpkin seeds, cilantro, cumin, remaining ½ teaspoon of oil, and ¼ teaspoon salt. Slice pork and serve with pesto poured over the top.

Stirred Eggs for Breakfast

Serves 4

Serve these elegant scrambled eggs with any muffins. Cheddar, Swiss, or goat cheese can be substituted for the fontina, while crispy cooked bacon or pancetta can stand in for the prosciutto.

- 8 eggs, blended
- 2 tablespoons milk
- Salt and pepper
- 1 tablespoon butter
- ¼ cup finally diced fontina cheese
- ¼ cup finely shredded prosciutto
- 1 tablespoon finely chopped fresh chives

In bowl, whisk blended eggs. Pour through fine mesh sieve into another bowl. Make sure white stringy parts remain in sieve. Add milk, salt, and pepper. In skillet, melt butter over medium heat. Add eggs and using wooden spoon, stir continuously. As the egg begins to form curds, keep stirring until very creamy, 3 minutes longer. Add cheese and prosciutto, continuing to stir until eggs form thicker curds but are still creamy. Garnish with chives when serving.

Salmon Teriyaki

Serves 6-8

- 1 quart soy sauce
- 1 pound brown sugar
- 1 teaspoon dry mustard
- 2 garlic cloves, minced
- ½ cup white wine
- 3 tablespoons sesame seeds (toasted is okay)
- 6 salmon fillets, 8 oz each

Mix marinade by combining first six ingredients. Place fillets in the marinade for 4 to 6 hours. Grill fillets 4-10 minutes or until milky white substance appears and fish flakes.

Just delicious!

Better Than Sex Cake

Makes a 9 x 13-inch cake

This is a cake I made for the ladies' get-together when our men were deployed and it was such a hit. From my military officers' wives' club dessert recipe. Enjoy!

First layer (crust):

- 1 stick butter
- 1 cup flour
- 1 cup chopped walnuts

Combine and spread in greased 9 x 13-inch glass baking pan. Bake at 350°F for 20 minutes and cool.

Second layer:

- 1 8-oz package cream cheese
- 1 8-oz container Cool Whip
- 1 cup powdered sugar

Mix and spread on cool crust. Refrigerate to chill.

Third layer:

- 2 small boxes instant chocolate pudding
- 3 cups milk
- Additional 8-oz container Cool Whip for topping

Mix instant pudding and milk for 3 minutes with electric mixer and spread on chilled cream cheese layer. Refrigerate.

Top with 8 oz Cool Whip right before serving. I made this so often and everyone was amazed.

Just decadence! Your guests will be speechless, as it should be.

Zebra Brownies

From my recipes as an officer's wife. I often made this dessert that would last only a couple of days. In our chain of command, when a family went home with a newborn baby, I delivered a full course meal the day they went home. A batch of these brownies went to every new mother and father.

Filling:

- 2 3-oz packages cream cheese, softened
- ¼ cup sugar
- ½ teaspoon vanilla
- 1 egg

Brownies:

- 1 package fudge brownie mix
- ⅓ cup water
- ⅓ cup olive oil
- 1 egg

Preheat oven to 350°F.

Spray 9-inch square pan with Pam. In bowl, beat filling ingredients until smooth. Set aside. In large bowl, combine all brownie ingredients. Spread half of brownie mixture then pour cream cheese filling on top in spoonfuls. Place remaining brownie batter on top of cream cheese. Spoon remaining cream cheese filling on top. Marble by pulling knife through batter with wide turns.

Bake for 30 to 35 minutes until set. Do not overbake! Cool completely. Cut into squares and refrigerate.

Pig Lickin' (Picken) Cake

Makes a 9 x 13-inch cake

This is another dessert from Ozark, Alabama, from my military wife days.

Cake:

- 1 yellow cake mix
- 4 eggs
- ¾ cup olive oil
- 1 11-oz can mandarin oranges in juice (do not drain)

Preheat oven to 350°F.

Mix all ingredients for cake in large bowl by hand. Bake for 20-25 minutes. Cool.

Icing:

- 1 3¾-oz box instant vanilla pudding mix
- 1 15½-oz can crushed pineapple with juice
- 1 8-oz container frozen Cool Whip

Mix all by hand, spread on cooled cake, and refrigerate until ready to serve.

Crab Martini

Serves 4-6

This makes an impressive presentation as a starter for any meal. Takes the place of salad.

- 12-15 fresh asparagus stalks
- 1 cup mayonnaise
- 2 tablespoons spicy or Dijon mustard
- 2-3 small tomatoes, diced
- Zest and juice of 1 lemon, plus more for dipping martini glasses
- 1 pound lump crab meat, cleaned, picked, and cooked
- Lemon pepper seasoning
- Seasoning salt
- House seasoning (see recipe that follows)
- Crab boil seasoning (recommend Old Bay)
- Lemon wedges for garnish
- Olives for garnish

You can serve individually in martini glasses or in any beautiful glass of your choice.

Boil asparagus in water to blanch for 1 minute, then transfer to a bowl of ice water. Cut off the tops of asparagus (2 inches) and set aside for garnish. Finely chop the remaining asparagus. In medium bowl, combine chopped asparagus with mayonnaise, mustard, tomatoes, lemon zest, and lemon juice. Gently fold the crab meat into the asparagus mixture and season to taste with lemon pepper, seasoning salt, and house seasoning.

Using the extra lemon juice, wet the rim of the martini glass and dip into the crab boil seasoning (it's almost the same as putting salt on the rim of a margarita glass).

Put crab mixture into prepared glass and serve with asparagus tops, lemon wedges, and olives as garnish. Chill until ready to serve.

House seasoning:

- 1 cup salt
- ¼ cup black pepper
- ¼ cup garlic powder

Mix ingredients together and store in airtight container up to six months. Only use house seasoning in crab mixture, 1 tablespoon at a time, to taste.

Ice Cream Pie

Serves 4-8

Crust:

- Oreo cookies (two rows of small bag)
- ½ cup butter, melted
- Small amount of milk

Remove white cream from inside of cookies. Place chocolate cookies in large Ziploc bag and crush into crumbs. In bowl with Oreo crumbs, add melted butter and small amount of milk. Mix. Press into 9-inch pie pan. Set aside.

Filling:

- 2 quarts Dreyer's (or Edy's, depending on where you live) coffee ice cream, softened slightly
- Hershey's fudge topping

Place softened ice cream into pie pan on top of Oreo crust, piled high. Spread fudge topping over ice cream and freeze until ready to serve.

Vegetable Bars

Makes about 2 dozen

These are my most treasured appetizers and I often serve them during holidays and at family get-togethers. They are so special, they will disappear! Your guests will think you spent hours in the kitchen.

Bake:

- 2 packages Pillsbury crescent roll dough

Unroll and push them together on a cookie sheet to make a continuous layer. Bake 8-10 minutes, per package directions. Set aside. Let cool.

Next, place in a bowl:

- 2 8-oz packages cream cheese, softened
- 1 package Hidden Valley dressing dry mix
- ¾ cup mayonnaise
- 1 teaspoon garlic salt

Mix all together and spread over baked crust in a thin layer with spatula.

Topping (shred or dice all, very thin and tiny):

- 1 large firm tomato
- 2 stalks green onions
- ¼ bunch fresh broccoli (cut tops with kitchen scissors)
- 1 carrot, shredded on smallest size
- ¾ block sharp cheddar cheese

Mix topping ingredients and spread on cream cheese mixture. Chill two hours in refrigerator. Cut into squares and arrange on platter. Chill until ready to serve.

Note: The topping colors look beautiful together. Remember all toppings should be cut very tiny. Press the veggies with the palm of your hand lightly into the cream cheese before slicing (the topping will stay better since it tends to fall off). Cut squares into brownie size, not too small. Use a beautiful platter of any color to serve.

These are my family's very favorite. They have become a family tradition!

Salmon Quinoa Burgers and Arugula Salad

Makes 5 patties

Patties:

- 16 oz wild salmon filet (skin removed), chopped
- 1 teaspoon olive oil
- ⅓ cup shallots, sliced
- 1 cup kale, chopped
- Salt and freshly cracked pepper
- ¾ cup cooked quinoa
- 2 tablespoons Dijon mustard
- ½ teaspoon Old Bay seasoning
- 1 large egg, beaten

Salad:

- 2½ tablespoons olive oil
- 2½ tablespoons champagne vinegar
- 2 tablespoons minced shallots
- 1¼ teaspoons Dijon mustard
- Salt and pepper
- 10 loosely packed cups arugula, washed and spun dry
- 1 large pink grapefruit, peeled and diced

In bowl, whisk oil, vinegar, shallots, Dijon mustard, salt, and pepper to make vinaigrette dressing. In food processor, finely chop 4 oz of the chopped salmon (this will hold burgers together). Heat oil, shallots, kale, salt, and pepper together for 4-5 minutes. Blend finely chopped salmon, remaining salmon, and cooked shallot and kale mixture together and form into patties. These can be grilled or cooked in a skillet on the stove.

Place arugula in large salad bowl. Dress with vinaigrette and top with diced grapefruit. Serve with salmon patties.

Rice Igaly Bogaly

Serves 4-6

Compliments of Martha Exley.

On Christmas Eve, a family tradition was to cook this dish after preparing so much for the Christmas dinner. The next day this was Grandma Martha Exley's tradition. We were tired after baking pies and making side dishes. We would have cocktails and play cards to relax. My husband and I spent Christmas Eve with Grandma Exley each year. These were very special moments, as Grandma was our queen. Grandma set all the standards of love and was an amazing woman. She loved her family with all her heart.

- 1 pound hamburger
- 2 cans La Choy oriental noodles (not dry noodles, with sauce)
- 1 can bean sprouts or fresh sprouts
- Soy sauce to your liking
- Water and cornstarch for thickening
- Freshly cooked white rice for serving

Brown hamburger in skillet. Add noodles, bean sprouts, and soy sauce and heat through. Mix together about 1 tablespoon cornstarch with a little water and add to pan, cooking until thickened.

Serve over white rice.

Best memories ever!

Mama Kitty's Zucchini Loaf

Makes 2 loaves

- 3 eggs
- 1 cup oil
- 2 cups sugar
- 2 teaspoons cinnamon
- 2 cups zucchini, grated
- 1 teaspoon vanilla
- 3 cups flour
- 1 teaspoon nutmeg
- ¼ teaspoon baking powder
- 1 teaspoon baking soda
- 1 teaspoon salt

Preheat oven to 350°F.

Mix all ingredients together in a large bowl. Separate into 2 greased loaf pans. Bake for 1 hour and 15 minutes.

My New York Cheesecake

Serves 8-10

Homemade by Mary Sue.

Crust:

* 1½ cups graham cracker crumbs
* ⅔ stick of butter, melted

Blend cracker crumbs and butter and place into a well buttered 9-inch spring-form pan. Press into bottom and sides to form crust.

Cheesecake mixture:

* 4 eggs, beaten
* 1 cup sugar
* 3 8-oz packages cream cheese
* 1 teaspoon vanilla
* Pinch of salt

Preheat oven to 350°F.

Mix cheesecake ingredients well for 20 minutes with electric mixer. Pour over crust in pan. Bake for 35 minutes. Cool for 10 minutes before adding topping.

Topping:

* 2 teaspoons sugar
* 1 pint sour cream
* ½ teaspoon vanilla extract

Adjust oven temperature to 375°F.

Mix topping ingredients together well. Spread over top of baked cheese-cake and bake for 7-10 minutes at 375°F until set (more likely a full 10 minutes). Let cool and refrigerate until ready to serve. Make a day ahead to improve flavor.

Enjoy!

Million Dollar Chicken

Serves 8

After graduation from Boise State University, we were off to flight school/Army aviation at Fort Rucker, Alabama. Yes, we earned our aviation wings in Ozark, Alabama. It was amazing!

- 8 chicken breasts
- 1 cup mayonnaise
- ½ cup mango chutney
- 1 tablespoon French's mustard
- ¼ cup Smucker's apricot jam
- ¾ cup water
- 1 package Lipton Onion Soup and Dip Mix

Preheat oven to 350°F.

Place the chicken in a casserole dish. Mix all other ingredients together. Pour over chicken. Bake for 60 minutes.

Serve with a side salad or steamed veggies of choice.

Southern Fried Chicken Ozark, Alabama Style

Best if fried in a cast-iron skillet.

- Chicken parts with skin (legs, thighs, wings, breasts)
- Flour
- Corn flakes
- Cayenne pepper, black pepper, crushed Himalayan salt, and garlic powder to taste for seasoning flour
- Buttermilk for dipping

Season flour to taste. Blend equal parts with crushed corn flakes and place in a bowl.

Heat oil (note: use Wesson Oil—it's the best) in a cast-iron skillet and follow these steps:

Put chicken pieces in bowl of ice water to get any blood out.

Pat dry.

Dip into a bowl of buttermilk.

Dredge lightly with equal parts seasoned flour and crushed corn flakes.

Repeat buttermilk dip and dredge in flour steps 4-5 times.

Place into a cast-iron skillet, making sure oil is hot.

Do not move chicken around much. Place on a brown paper bag to drain and cool.

Enjoy. Best chicken ever!

Pesto Shrimp Salad

Serves 6-8

Everyone loves shrimp, especially me. Premade, purchased pesto is best for this dish. Sometimes I have to double this dish as my family goes crazy over it.

- 2 pounds uncooked large shrimp, peeled and deveined
- 3 tablespoons crab boil seasoning
- ½ cup prepared basil pesto
- 1 stalk celery, finally chopped
- ¼ cup mayonnaise
- ¼ cup finely chopped red bell pepper
- 3 tablespoons finely chopped red onion
- Salt and freshly ground cracked pepper
- Mixed salad greens

In large pot, add shrimp and crab boil seasoning. Toss to coat. Fill with water and cover shrimp by 2 inches. Heat on medium for 8 minutes. Cover and let stand 2 to 3 minutes. Drain. In large bowl, toss shrimp, pesto, celery, mayonnaise, red bell pepper, and onion. Season with salt and freshly cracked pepper. Serve at room temperature or chilled on a bed of mixed greens.

This is one of my all-time favorites! Amazing.

Angie's Goulash

Serves 8-10

This is such an amazing recipe for family nights or any celebration. It makes a giant pot. Let me tell you, there are no leftovers.

- 2 tablespoons extra virgin olive oil
- 2 pounds ground beef
- 1 12-oz package Jimmy Dean sausage, "maple flavor"
- 2 large onions (sweet is best)
- 2 14½-oz cans diced tomatoes
- 1 29-oz can tomato sauce
- 3 tablespoons soy sauce
- 2 teaspoons dried basil
- 2 teaspoons dried oregano
- 3 cloves fresh garlic, minced
- 1 teaspoon garlic powder or garlic salt
- ¾ teaspoon salt and fresh ground pepper
- 2 cups uncooked elbow macaroni

In large Dutch oven pot, add oil and brown all meats for 10 minutes. Add onion and stir and cook 5 minutes. Add remaining ingredients except macaroni. Cover and simmer for 20 minutes. Stir in macaroni, cover again, and simmer for another 20 minutes.

Let stand for 20 minutes before serving in bowls. Fresh bread of your choice can be served with this dish. I recommend Dutch crunch!

This is an amazing dish that everyone loves.

Southern Style Corned Beef and Cabbage

My daddy was full Irish. He would be so proud of how I perfected this dish with love.

- 1 4-pound corned beef brisket
- 3 cloves garlic
- ½ teaspoon hot sauce—I use fRed Sauce (the label says "Eat with Passion")
- 2 bay leaves
- Pickling spices wrapped in cheesecloth and tied with rubber band or string—add to boiling water
- 4-8 slices of bacon
- 1 head green cabbage, cut into four wedges
- 4 potatoes (1½ pounds), peeled and halved
- Mustard

Rinse corn beef and place in a large pot. Add garlic, bay leaves, tied pickling spices, and enough water to cover. Bring to a boil and simmer for 4 hours. Cook bacon until crisp and set aside. Using bacon drippings, cook cabbage wedges and potatoes in batches over medium heat until brown but not tender. Transfer beef to platter and cover with foil. Using cooking water from beef, add the potatoes and cook 15 minutes. Add cabbage and simmer 15 more minutes. Discard bay leaves and tied spices. Transfer vegetables to platter with slotted spoon. Crumble bacon over all. Serve with mustard.

Fred's Bloody Marys

Makes 6 cocktails

Fred created his own Bloody Mary recipe. He makes them spicy, light, and with the most amazing taste. Fred is the owner of his very own fRed red pepper sauce. Do not substitute hot sauce. It must be the one and only fRed Sauce. Order at fredsauce.com. It's made in Bend, Oregon, and is organic.

- 3 cups tomato juice
- ¾ cup vodka
- 2 tablespoons freshly squeezed lime juice
- 1½ teaspoons fRed Sauce
- 1½ teaspoons Worcestershire sauce
- ½ teaspoon onion salt
- ½ teaspoon celery seeds
- Four green onions
- Green olives

In a pitcher, mix together all of the ingredients except green onions and green olives. Place a bunch of green olives in bottom of tall glasses and add ice on top. Pour Mary mixture into the glasses. Garnish with green onions.

This Bloody Mary is the best I have ever had.

Prosciutto and Asparagus Baby Spinach Salad

Serves 4

This salad delivers the most fantastic taste—it's my absolute favorite. When I really want to entertain, this is it. I like to serve on chilled salad plates. This can also be a main dish for Sunday brunch with a glass of prosecco.

- 2 bundles asparagus, cooked very al dente/crunchy
- 12 slices prosciutto
- 6 Roma tomatoes, halved
- Olive oil
- Cracked black pepper
- 6½ oz baby spinach leaves
- 1 cup shaved Parmesan cheese (I use a long grater—I prefer long slices, tossed in salad)

Dressing:

- 2 tablespoons olive oil
- 2 tablespoons lemon juice
- 1 cup basil leaves, shredded
- 2 teaspoons brown sugar

Preheat oven to 350°F.

Place prosciutto and tomatoes on baking sheet. Sprinkle with olive oil and cracked black pepper. Bake 25 minutes until the prosciutto is crisp and to-matoes are soft. Arrange the spinach and asparagus in a large serving bowl or arrange on plates. Top with tomatoes, broken up pieces of prosciutto, and Parmesan. Blend dressing ingredients, pour over salad, and serve fresh.

Scallops with Watercress

Serves 6-8

The fresh and vibrant color of the sauce combined with the delicate texture of the scallops makes this a most inviting, as well as delicious, first course.

- ½ cup dry vermouth
- ½ onion, sliced (sweet white or Walla Walla)
- Sprig of fresh parsley, Italian flat leaf variety
- One bay leaf
- Salt and freshly cracked pepper to taste
- 1 pound sea scallops, cut in half (I use jumbo Trader Joe's)
- Boston lettuce for serving

In large saucepan, heat vermouth, onion, parsley, bay leaf, salt, and black pepper. Add scallops and simmer gently until just cooked through, 5 to 7 minutes, stirring occasionally with wooden spoon. Do not overcook! Remove scallops to separate bowl. Cover scallops in plastic wrap and refrigerate. Reserve broth with onion and parsley for soups or stocks.

Watercress sauce:
- 1 cup mayonnaise
- ½ cup watercress, chopped
- ¼ cup Italian parsley
- ¼ cup chives or scallions, chopped
- 1½ teaspoons fresh dill, chopped
- 2 teaspoons lemon juice or lime juice (I prefer lime)

In an electric blender, combine all sauce ingredients and blend until smooth. Chill sauce in blender in refrigerator. On individual plates, place Boston lettuce and then scallops evenly divided on top with sauce. Garnish with watercress or parsley. Serve immediately.

Tenderloin Deluxe

Serves 8

For your most distinguished guests. So elegant. Complements any side dish.

- 3 pounds whole beef tenderloin
- 2 tablespoons softened butter
- ¼ cup chopped scallions
- 2 tablespoons butter
- 2 tablespoons soy sauce
- 1 teaspoon Dijon wine mustard
- Cracked black pepper
- ¾ cup dry sherry
- ½ bunch chopped fresh Italian parsley

For best results, the meat should sit at room temperature for 2 to 3 hours before roasting. Preheat oven to 400°F.

Spread the tenderloin with softened butter. Place on a rack in roasting pan and bake uncovered for 20 minutes. Meanwhile, make the sauce: sauté the scallions in remaining butter until tender. Add soy sauce, mustard, and cracked pepper. Stir in dry sherry and heat just until boiling.

When the meat has baked 20 minutes, pour the sauce over it and bake another 20 to 25 minutes to serve medium rare. Baste frequently. Remove from oven and let sit 10 minutes, then carve into 1-inch slices, overlapping them attractively on platter. Lavish with chopped parsley. Pour sauce over meat and serve.

Risotto Alla Milanese

Serves 6-8

A most elegant risotto. It is delicious and versatile, and complements the most formal as well as casual menus. This is one of my favorites.

- 5 tablespoons butter
- 1 sweet white onion, chopped
- 1 cup dry white wine
- 2 cups white risotto rice or long grain white rice
- 1 teaspoon salt
- ¼ teaspoon white pepper
- ½ teaspoon saffron threads
- 4-5 cups chicken broth
- 3 tablespoons butter
- 1 cup freshly grated Parmesan cheese

Melt 5 tablespoons butter in 4-quart saucepan and add onion. Cook, stirring constantly, until transparent but not brown. And wine and cook until evaporated. Add rice, salt, and white pepper, and stir until every grain is covered with butter. Add saffron and about 2 cups chicken broth. Cook to let liquid almost completely evaporate before adding remaining broth, a little at a time. Reduce heat and continue to cook, uncovered and stirring frequently, for about 20 to 25 minutes or until it has reached the "al dente" stage. Remove from heat and add remaining butter plus several tablespoons of grated cheese.

Place remaining cheese in a serving bowl for those guests who wish extra.

Kona Inn Banana Bread

Makes 2 loaves

This is an absolute must serve with any salad for a first course. It's the best banana bread, as it stays moist indefinitely—although it is always gone before we can prove that fact!

- 2 cups granulated sugar
- 1 cup softened butter
- 6 ripe bananas, smashed (approximately 3 cups)
- 4 eggs, well beaten
- 2½ cups cake flour
- 2 teaspoons baking soda
- 1 teaspoon salt

Preheat oven to 350°F.

With electric beater, cream together sugar and butter until light and fluffy. Add bananas and eggs, beating until well mixed.

Sift together dry ingredients 3 times. Blend with banana mixture but do not over mix.

Pour into lightly greased 9-inch loaf pans. Bake for 45 minutes to 1 hour, until firm in the center and the edges begin to separate from the pan.

Cool on a rack for 10 minutes before removing from pans. These freeze beautifully.

Asparagus Rolls

Makes 75

Both the appearance and the taste of these are so beautiful. Period. Truly a superb hors d'oeuvre. Since these are made ahead of time, it makes them lovely to serve at dinner parties or holiday gatherings.

- 25 fresh asparagus spears
- Salt to taste
- 25 thin slices white bread
- 8 oz cream cheese, softened
- 3 oz blue cheese, softened
- 1 egg
- ¾ pound butter, melted

In skillet, bring enough water to boil to barely cover asparagus. Trim spears to same length as bread slices and place in skillet. Sprinkle with salt and parsley and cover with a lid. Boil gently until parts of stalks are barely fork tender, 3 to 5 minutes, depending on size of stalk. Drain immediately and rinse in cold water until cooking process has ended.

Remove crusts from bread and flatten with rolling pin. Combine both cheeses and egg with an electric mixer. Spread mixture evenly over bread slices. Place an asparagus spear on each one and roll up. Dip in melted butter to coat all sides.

Place on cookie sheet and freeze until ready to bake. Preheat oven to 400°F. Cut frozen rolls into thirds and bake, still frozen, for 15 minutes until browned. Serve immediately.

California Orange Soup

Serves 10 to 12

Pretty refreshing. Period. The most unusual soup for a summer luncheon or brunch. On a hot day, serve as a first course or feature in frosted wine goblets with molasses crisps as an evening dessert. I have tried both. Your compliments!

- 4½ cups fresh orange juice
- 1 cup fresh lemon juice
- 2 tablespoons sugar
- 2 tablespoons quick-cooking tapioca
- Dash of salt
- 2 cinnamon sticks
- 4 cups fresh sliced peaches
- 1 cup sugar
- ¼ cup flour
- ¼ teaspoon cinnamon
- 1½ cups orange sections
- 1 banana, sliced
- ¼ cup Cointreau liqueur (optional)
- Sour cream (optional)
- ½ pint fresh raspberries

Combine the orange juice and lemon juice, 2 tablespoons sugar, tapioca, and salt in large saucepan. Let stand five minutes. Add cinnamon sticks and bring to a boil over medium heat. Let simmer for 5 minutes, uncovered, stirring occasionally.

Combine sliced peaches, sugar, flour, and cinnamon. Add to pan and simmer another 5 minutes, stirring from time to time. Remove from heat and let cool.

Cut orange slice sections into bite-sized pieces, removing any membranes. Add to cool soup with sliced bananas and Cointreau. Remove cinnamon sticks and chill well.

To serve, ladle into chilled soup bowls or chilled goblets. If you wish, garnish each with a tablespoon of sour cream and a few fresh raspberries.

Note: If preparing a day in advance, do not add banana slices until several hours before serving. Serve chilled.

Molasses Crisps

Makes 8 dozen

These are like lace cookies but easy to handle and certainly delicious. The dough keeps well in the refrigerator or freezer for last-minute treats. Serve with California orange soup as an elegant evening dessert.

- ¾ cup oatmeal
- ¾ cup sifted flour
- 1 cup sugar
- ½ teaspoon baking powder
- ¼ teaspoon salt
- 1 teaspoon cinnamon
- ¼ teaspoon ground cloves
- ½ cup butter, melted
- ¼ cup milk or half-and-half
- ¼ cup light molasses

Preheat oven to 350°F.

Combine dry ingredients and spices. Combine melted butter, milk, and molasses. Stir liquid into dry ingredients until smooth. Chill for easier handling.

Oil foil-lined cookie sheets. Drop batter by ½ teaspoon, 3 to 4 inches apart (9 cookies per sheet). Bake for 8 to 10 minutes. Let cool a half minute on cookie sheet before removing with spatula to a rack to cool completely.

About the Author

April May Thomas's children are who she values most in this world. Her recipes have been the inspiration for connecting with family and friends for conversations, laughter, and tears. When April cooks, it's not just about the food. Being in the kitchen is her favorite, most important part of her day. She pours love and creativity into her gift of providing life, nourishment, and relief from stress for those she loves. As her daughter, Jen, says, "When my mom comes home to cook for me, it brings me peace, feeds my soul, and heals my heart."

April grew up surrounded by amazing cooks—her grandmother, her aunts, and her mother. As the youngest of three, she was close with her mother and loved being in the kitchen to learn cooking traditions, passion, and skill from her. Some of April's favorite chefs are great role models like Joanna Gaines, Lidia Bastianich, and Julia Child.

April graduated from Boise State University and moved to Fort Rucker in Ozark, Alabama, where her husband attended Army flight school. She served as president of the officers' wives' club, and she loved the cooking and charm of the South and being called "Miss April." Her experiences with the Army in Alabama and across the world, as she and her husband traveled for his assignments, contributed to her rich cooking expertise.

She loved gospel music, writing music, and singing—and Elvis Presley's singing was just *it* for her. While her first dream career of being a famous singer didn't come to be, she did have three minutes of fame when she got a chance to sing "Ring of Fire" on stage with Johnny Cash and earned a standing ovation.

April is fearless in the kitchen and in life. She had a chance to drive a Porsche 911 Turbo in wheel to wheel racing and discovered an unexpected talent. She saw the cracks in the wall many times but never wrecked. Her children always came to the track with her. She won regularly and her car was once featured on the cover of *Road & Track* magazine.

Leadership and effective business management come naturally to April, which she learned when she bought a failing day spa in Bend, Oregon, while she was raising her children. She applied all her dental practice consulting skills and took the business from 13 to 48 full-time employees and sold the business at a substantial profit three years later.

She embraced the community while she was there, and offered full-day make-overs to one homeless woman each month. Each woman's special day included massage, facial, a catered lunch on china, and hair color and style. They were then sent out into the world to apply for jobs. One woman said, "When I left your spa, I took a piece of my self-esteem that nobody could buy." She also provided free haircuts to any elementary school child who needed one, bringing them into the spa before picture day.

Throughout her life, she has provided her children with family dinners by candlelight to offer a safe place, no matter what was happening. In the rush of modern life, it's easy to forget the joys of home-cooked food and the importance of passing these values down to children and grandchildren. Her recipes are meant to help anyone learn to cook at home. April has compiled treasured recipes over the past four decades of travel, cooking, and sharing comfort and love.

Notes

Notes

Notes

"Before Elvis, there was nothing."

—John Lennon

9 781612 062204